# Proverbs 31 Woman Bible Study & Companion Workbook

Angelica K. Duncan

Silk Over Steel, LLC

# Proverbs 31 Woman Bible Study And Companion Workbook

*More Than A Checklist: A 15-Day Devotional To Discover Biblical Truths About The Virtuous Woman*

Angelica K. Duncan

© 2019 Silk Over Steel, LLC

All rights reserved. No part of this publication may be reproduced, stored in a retrieval system or transmitted in any form or by any means, electronic, mechanical, photocopying, recording or otherwise without the prior permission of the publisher or in accordance with the provisions of the Copyright, Designs and Patents Act 1988 or under the terms of any licence permitting limited copying issued by the Copyright Licensing Agency.

Unless otherwise stated, Scripture quotations are from The ESV® Bible (The Holy Bible, English Standard Version®), copyright © 2001 by Crossway, a publishing ministry of Good News Publishers. Used by permission. All rights reserved.

**Published by:**
Silk Over Steel, LLC
Post Office Box 5001
High Point, NC 27262

A CIP record for this book is available from the Library of Congress Cataloging-in-Publication Data

**ISBN-10:** 1 69381 454 4

**ISBN-13:** 978 1 69381 454 9

Printed in USA

# Table of Contents

**Day 1**
Introduction: It's All About Your Character . . . . . . . . . . . . . . . . . . . . . . . . . . . . . . . . 5

**Day 2**
The Meaning of Virtuous . . . . . . . . . . . . . . . . . . . . . . . . . . . . . . . . . . . . . . . . . . . . .13

**Day 3**
You Are His Good Thing! . . . . . . . . . . . . . . . . . . . . . . . . . . . . . . . . . . . . . . . . . . . . .21

**Day 4**
A Willing, Eager Worker . . . . . . . . . . . . . . . . . . . . . . . . . . . . . . . . . . . . . . . . . . . . . 29

**Day 5**
Going The Distance For Your Loved Ones . . . . . . . . . . . . . . . . . . . . . . . . . . . . . . 37

**Day 6**
Being Mrs. Organized . . . . . . . . . . . . . . . . . . . . . . . . . . . . . . . . . . . . . . . . . . . . . . . 45

**Day 7**
Use Your Skills & Resourcefulness To Bless Your Family . . . . . . . . . . . . . . . . . . 53

**Day 8**
Know The Worth Of Your Work! . . . . . . . . . . . . . . . . . . . . . . . . . . . . . . . . . . . . . . 61

**Day 9**
Creating A Legacy of Philanthropy . . . . . . . . . . . . . . . . . . . . . . . . . . . . . . . . . . . . 69

**Day 10**
Being Prepared For The Seasons In Life . . . . . . . . . . . . . . . . . . . . . . . . . . . . . . . . 77

**Day 11**
Your Impact On Your Man . . . . . . . . . . . . . . . . . . . . . . . . . . . . . . . . . . . . . . . . . . . 85

**Day 12**
The Freedom To Be Enterprising . . . . . . . . . . . . . . . . . . . . . . . . . . . . . . . . . . . . . . 93

**Day 13**
Speak Wisdom, Kindness, & Life! . . . . . . . . . . . . . . . . . . . . . . . . . . . . . . . . . . . . . 101

**Day 14**
Let Your Children & Husband Praise You! . . . . . . . . . . . . . . . . . . . . . . . . . . . . . . 109

**Day 15**
The One Thing That Matters Most (Eternity) . . . . . . . . . . . . . . . . . . . . . . . . . . . . 117

# Welcome to our Proverbs 31 Woman Online Bible Study!

I'm so glad you're here, SisterFriend!

Thank you for joining me and over 100,000 women from across the globe, as we focus in becoming a Proverbs 31 Woman. I pray that your heart is open and your spirit is ready for the transformation the Holy Spirit will bring. May your faithfulness meet its full reward!

**You can register for this Bible Study and find all of the materials and resources I have you right here!**
https://proverbs31businesswoman.com/p31biblestudy

For this Bible Study, we are going to use the S.O.A.P. Method, as we dig into God's Word.

### What is S.O.A.P.?

S.O.A.P. stands for Scripture, Observation, Application and Prayer. It is a way of getting more out of your time in God's word. I didn't invent it, but I find it very helpful to use. You don't have to have be a theologian, in order to study God's word – you just need desire and commitment. The S.O.A.P. Method makes it super simple for the expert and novice alike to get meaning out of the Bible.

### How does it work?

It's quite simple! When you sit for your daily quiet time, read the bible as you normally would with one simple difference - underline or make note of any verses that pull at your heartstrings. This is the basis for diving deeper and using S.O.A.P.

Here's how you'll complete your workbook page for each day:

### Scripture

Write down the scripture that tugs at your heartstrings the most.

### Observation

What did you observe about the scripture that struck you? This can be one sentence or a whole book.

### Application

How can you apply this deeper meaning so that it affects your life today?

### Prayer

Write out a prayer to God based on what you just learned and ask him to help you apply this truth in your life.

Thank you for joining me! :)

**Dance with the King!**

*Angelica*

# Bible Reading Plan

## Week 1

- ☐ Day 1 — Proverbs 31:10-31
- ☐ Day 2 — Proverbs 31:10
- ☐ Day 3 — Proverbs 31:11-12
- ☐ Day 4 — Proverbs 31:13
- ☐ Day 5 — Proverbs 31:14

## Week 2

- ☐ Day 6 — Proverbs 31:15
- ☐ Day 7 — Proverbs 31:16
- ☐ Day 8 — Proverbs 31:17-18
- ☐ Day 9 — Proverbs 31:19-20
- ☐ Day 10 — Proverbs 31:21-22

## Week 3

- ☐ Day 11 — Proverbs 31:23
- ☐ Day 12 — Proverbs 31:24-25
- ☐ Day 13 — Proverbs 31:26-27
- ☐ Day 14 — Proverbs 31:28-29
- ☐ Day 15 — Proverbs 31:30-31

DAY 1

# Introduction: It's All About Your Character

*Proverbs 31:10-31*

<sup>10</sup> An excellent wife who can find? She is far more precious than jewels.

<sup>11</sup> The heart of her husband trusts in her, and he will have no lack of gain.

<sup>12</sup> She does him good, and not harm, all the days of her life.

<sup>13</sup> She seeks wool and flax, and works with willing hands.

<sup>14</sup> She is like the ships of the merchant; she brings her food from afar.

<sup>15</sup> She rises while it is yet night and provides food for her household and portions for her maidens.

<sup>16</sup> She considers a field and buys it; with the fruit of her hands she plants a vineyard.

<sup>17</sup> She dresses herself with strength and makes her arms strong.

<sup>18</sup> She perceives that her merchandise is profitable. Her lamp does not go out at night.

<sup>19</sup> She puts her hands to the distaff, and her hands hold the spindle.

<sup>20</sup> She opens her hand to the poor and reaches out her hands to the needy.

<sup>21</sup> She is not afraid of snow for her household, for all her household are clothed in scarlet.

<sup>22</sup> She makes bed coverings for herself; her clothing is fine linen and purple.

<sup>23</sup> Her husband is known in the gates when he sits among the elders of the land.

<sup>24</sup> She makes linen garments and sells them; she delivers sashes to the merchant.

<sup>25</sup> Strength and dignity are her clothing, and she laughs at the time to come.

<sup>26</sup> She opens her mouth with wisdom, and the teaching of kindness is on her tongue.

<sup>27</sup> She looks well to the ways of her household and does not eat the bread of idleness.

<sup>28</sup> Her children rise up and call her blessed; her husband also, and he praises her:

<sup>29</sup> "Many women have done excellently, but you surpass them all."

<sup>30</sup> Charm is deceitful, and beauty is vain, but a woman who fears the Lord is to be praised.

<sup>31</sup> Give her of the fruit of her hands, and let her works praise her in the gates.

# SOAP Scripture Study
# Day 1

## Video Lesson
https://proverbs31businesswoman.com/proverbs-31-woman-bible-study-day1

## Scripture
Write down today's focus scripture.

## Observation
What did you observe about the scripture that struck you?

## Application
How can you apply this deeper meaning, so that it has a heartfelt impact on your life?

## Prayer
Write out a prayer to God based upon what you just learned and where you'd like to grow, in your life.

# Notes & Journaling
# Day 1

# Notes & Journaling
# Day 1

# Notes & Journaling
# Day 1

# Reflections & Questions
# Day 1

1. As you've read or heard about the Proverbs 31 Woman what are your feelings about how you measure up to her character traits?

2. Have you taken the time to explain to your child(ren) the characteristics of a good and Godly spouse? Make a list of those qualities that you desire your child(ren) to find in a mate, pray about it, the begin teaching them!

3. Take a moment and evaluate yourself on the following. What are your areas for growth?

**Scriptural knowledge of following:**   0 = immature   5 = mature

| | |
|---|---|
| Fear of God | 0 1 2 3 4 5 |
| Holiness | 0 1 2 3 4 5 |
| Wisdom | 0 1 2 3 4 5 |
| Sow-Reap Law | 0 1 2 3 4 5 |

**Personal maturity in godly character:**   0 = immature   5 = mature

| | |
|---|---|
| Trustworthiness | 0 1 2 3 4 5 |
| Control of tongue | 0 1 2 3 4 5 |
| Humility | 0 1 2 3 4 5 |
| Wisdom | 0 1 2 3 4 5 |
| Peace of mind | 0 1 2 3 4 5 |
| Diligence | 0 1 2 3 4 5 |
| Benevolence | 0 1 2 3 4 5 |
| Health and appearance | 0 1 2 3 4 5 |
| Excellence | 0 1 2 3 4 5 |

DAY 2

# The Meaning of Virtuous

*Proverbs 31:10*

---

¹⁰ An excellent wife who can find?
She is far more precious than jewels.

---

### CONFESSION OF TRUTH

I am a virtuous woman.

I am a woman of valor.

I am more precious than rubies.

My life is purposefully precious and priceless! All because the Lord says so!

Today, I choose to walk with strength, fitness, health, integrity, uprightness, and to bring riches, wherever I go.

I am 100% feminine. I am 100% strong.

I am developing the character of a woman who is built like Silk Over Steel.

I decree and declare this over my life, as according to Proverbs 31:10

And it is so -- Amen.

# SOAP Scripture Study
# Day 2

## Video Lesson
https://proverbs31businesswoman.com/proverbs-31-woman-bible-study-day2

## Scripture
Write down today's focus scripture.

## Observation
What did you observe about the scripture that struck you?

## Application
How can you apply this deeper meaning, so that it has a heartfelt impact on your life?

## Prayer
Write out a prayer to God based upon what you just learned and where you'd like to grow, in your life.

# Notes & Journaling
# Day 2

# Notes & Journaling
# Day 2

# Notes & Journaling
# Day 2

# Reflections & Questions
## Day 2

1. What does the word "Virtuous" mean? Which of those traits are you currently cultivating? Which traits do you need to focus in and continue to cultivate?

2. How does this definition change your understanding of what it means to be a Virtuous Woman?

3. What is your worth? How do you view yourself? Read the following scriptures. How do they speak to you and what God says about your worth/value?

Psalm 139:14

Jeremiah 29:11

Zephaniah 3:17

**DAY 3**

# You Are His Good Thing!
### Proverbs 31:11-12

---

¹¹ The heart of her husband trusts in her,
and he will have no lack of gain.

¹² She does him good, and not harm,
all the days of her life.

---

### CONFESSION OF TRUTH

I am a "Good Thing" to my (future) husband.

I am a "Good Thing" to all whom I encounter.

I am trustworthy. I am loyal. I am a gift. I am a blessing.

Today, I choose to walk in the revelation of that knowledge and truth. I bring prosperity, great fortune, good welfare, and happiness to my (future) husband's life.

I also bring prosperity, great fortune, better welfare, and happiness to the lives of others.

My (future) husband's heart safely trusts in me and he has no lack of gain. I will always do my (future) husband good and not evil, all the days of my life.

He will see the Glory of the Lord revealed to him through my "goodness."

I decree and declare this over my life, as according to Proverbs 31:11-12

And it is so -- Amen.

# SOAP Scripture Study
# Day 3

## Video Lesson

https://proverbs31businesswoman.com/proverbs-31-woman-bible-study-day3

## Scripture

Write down today's focus scripture.

## Observation

What did you observe about the scripture that struck you?

## Application

How can you apply this deeper meaning, so that it has a heartfelt impact on your life?

## Prayer

Write out a prayer to God based upon what you just learned and where you'd like to grow, in your life.

# Notes & Journaling
# Day 3

# Notes & Journaling
# Day 3

# Notes & Journaling
# Day 3

# Reflections & Questions
## Day 3

1. What does it mean to bring your husband GOOD to his life? What are some practical ways you can bring GOODNESS to him?

2. Why is loyalty important as a woman and wife?

3. Evaluate yourself on trustworthiness and loyalty. Where do you need to grow more?

**Personal growth:**  0 = immature   5 = mature

Honesty          0 1 2 3 4 5
Discretion       0 1 2 3 4 5
Contentment      0 1 2 3 4 5
Dependability    0 1 2 3 4 5

DAY 4

# A Willing, Eager Worker

## Proverbs 31:13

---

¹³ She seeks wool and flax,
and works with willing hands.

---

### CONFESSION OF TRUTH

I am a willing, eager worker.

I am diligent in finding the best for my home and family.

I have a good attitude and holy perspective about my work.

My work is a gift and I find ways to enjoy the gift of work God has given me.

The focus of my work is the Lord. I work as if I'm working for Him.

Every day, I'm thankful for the gift of work.

I decree and declare this over my life, as according to Proverbs 31:13

And it is so -- Amen.

# SOAP Scripture Study
# Day 4

## Video Lesson
https://proverbs31businesswoman.com/proverbs-31-woman-bible-study-day4

## Scripture
Write down today's focus scripture.

## Observation
What did you observe about the scripture that struck you?

## Application
How can you apply this deeper meaning, so that it has a heartfelt impact on your life?

## Prayer
Write out a prayer to God based upon what you just learned and where you'd like to grow, in your life.

# Notes & Journaling
# Day 4

# Notes & Journaling
# Day 4

# Notes & Journaling
# Day 4

# Reflections & Questions
# Day 4

1. Why were wool and flax important I Hebrew/Jewish culture?

2. What are some important and high commodity areas in your life and that of your family? How can you improve your work ethic in this area?

3. What is your attitude towards work? Are you a willing eager worker? How does today's reading change your perspective of work (whether in your home or outside of your home)?

Colossians 3:23

Proverbs 14:23

Proverbs 10:4

Proverbs 12:11

Ecclesiastes 3:13

DAY 5

# Going The Distance For Your Loved Ones

### Proverbs 31:14

---

¹⁴ She is like the ships of the merchant; she brings her food from afar.

---

### CONFESSION OF TRUTH

I love my family and their needs are important to me.

I go to great lengths to nourish, nurture, and tend the needs of my family.

I am a woman who always has the best interests of my family in mind.

I am developing the character traits of commitment and dedication, even in the face of my feelings and personal challenges.

I keep a holy and righteous perspective of the priority of my family, in my life.

I decree and declare this over my life, as according to Proverbs 31:14

And it is so -- Amen.

# SOAP Scripture Study
# Day 5

## Video Lesson
https://proverbs31businesswoman.com/proverbs-31-woman-bible-study-day5

## Scripture
Write down today's focus scripture.

## Observation
What did you observe about the scripture that struck you?

## Application
How can you apply this deeper meaning, so that it has a heartfelt impact on your life?

## Prayer
Write out a prayer to God based upon what you just learned and where you'd like to grow, in your life.

# Notes & Journaling
# Day 5

# Notes & Journaling
# Day 5

# Notes & Journaling
# Day 5

# Reflections & Questions
# Day 5

1. What did merchant ships do in biblical times?

2. How far are you willing to go to take care of you and your family? Give an example.

3. List some ways you can go the extra mile for your husband, children, siblings, friends, extended family members in cultivating this character of diligence.

**DAY 6**

# Being Mrs. Organized

*Proverbs 31:15*

---

<sup>15</sup> She rises while it is yet night and provides food for her household and portions for her maidens.

---

### CONFESSION OF TRUTH

I am well-organized.

I am productive.

I run an efficient home.

I know how to delegate tasks to the best person who can get the job done.

I am not ashamed to ask for help because help is a gift to me. It frees me up to be productive in other areas of my life.

I have wisdom and a keen eye to know who is trustworthy and loyal to ask for help.

I decree and declare this over my life, as according to Proverbs 31:15

And it is so -- Amen.

# SOAP Scripture Study
# Day 6

## Video Lesson
https://proverbs31businesswoman.com/proverbs-31-woman-bible-study-day6

## Scripture
Write down today's focus scripture.

## Observation
What did you observe about the scripture that struck you?

## Application
How can you apply this deeper meaning, so that it has a heartfelt impact on your life?

## Prayer
Write out a prayer to God based upon what you just learned and where you'd like to grow, in your life.

# Notes & Journaling
# Day 6

# Notes & Journaling
## Day 6

# Notes & Journaling
# Day 6

# Reflections & Questions
# Day 6

1. How do you feel about asking for help? Do you have people in your life that you can call on, if you needed to? List their names and contact information (then put it in a safe place for the future.)

2. List 2-3 areas where you need help – wiving, homemaking, child-rearing, job/career, etc.

3. How do you feel about your organization? How does your organization affect the flow of your home?

DAY 7

# Use Your Skills & Resourcefulness To Bless Your Family
### Proverbs 31:16

---

¹⁶ She considers a field and buys it; with the fruit of her hands she plants a vineyard.

---

### CONFESSION OF TRUTH

I am resourceful.

I am skillful.

I am purposeful.

I will use my skills to bless my family.

I will be intentional about building up resources so that future generations will be blessed.

I know it's not just about me, but my children's children. (And my niece's nieces and my nephew's nephews and my mentee's mentees.)

I am a legacy-minded woman. Everything I do, I do with legacy on my mind!

I decree and declare this over my life, as according to Proverbs 31:16

And it is so -- Amen.

# SOAP Scripture Study
# Day 7

## Video Lesson
https://proverbs31businesswoman.com/proverbs-31-woman-bible-study-day7

## Scripture
Write down today's focus scripture.

## Observation
What did you observe about the scripture that struck you?

## Application
How can you apply this deeper meaning, so that it has a heartfelt impact on your life?

## Prayer
Write out a prayer to God based upon what you just learned and where you'd like to grow, in your life.

# Notes & Journaling
# Day 7

# Notes & Journaling
# Day 7

# Notes & Journaling
# Day 7

# Reflections & Questions
## Day 7

1. What are some of your skill sets? List ALL of the things you do well or that others say you do well. (You're going to be surprised at this list!!)

2. How can you use your skills and the things you do well to benefit your family, friends, community, etc.?

3. What skills you need to develop? What are some skills you would like to learn?

DAY 8

# Know The Worth Of Your Work!

### Proverbs 31:17-18

---

¹⁷ She dresses herself with strength
and makes her arms strong.

¹⁸ She perceives that her merchandise is profitable.
Her lamp does not go out at night.

---

### CONFESSION OF TRUTH

My work is valuable and worthy.

I am confident in my gifts, talents, and skills.

My place in the Kingdom of God is invaluable and priceless. There's no one who can do what I do because God created me for such a time as this.

I choose to rise up in that truth and bring Glory to God by the full, exhausted use of all He's put into me to pour out into the earth.

I walk in a Holy source of strength. It stems from joy unspeakable!

Daily I am becoming strong in my character, spirit-man, and soul.

My work brings me excitement, fulfillment, and joy!

I decree and declare this over my life, as according to Proverbs 31:17-18

And it is so -- Amen.

# SOAP Scripture Study
# Day 8

## Video Lesson
https://proverbs31businesswoman.com/proverbs-31-woman-bible-study-day8

## Scripture
Write down today's focus scripture.

## Observation
What did you observe about the scripture that struck you?

## Application
How can you apply this deeper meaning, so that it has a heartfelt impact on your life?

## Prayer
Write out a prayer to God based upon what you just learned and where you'd like to grow, in your life.

# Notes & Journaling
# Day 8

# Notes & Journaling
# Day 8

# Notes & Journaling
# Day 8

# Reflections & Questions
## Day 8

1. What does Godly strength mean to you? What are some ways you exemplify it?

2. What is your work worth? What value do you bring to your family, friends, community?

3. Now that we're halfway through our Proverbs 31 Online Bible Study what are some common themes in this woman's character you've noticed?

DAY 9

# Creating A Legacy of Philanthropy
## Proverbs 31:19-20

---

¹⁹ She puts her hands to the distaff,
and her hands hold the spindle.

²⁰ She opens her hand to the poor
and reaches out her hands to the needy.

---

**CONFESSION OF TRUTH**

I am a sower.

I am a giver.

I am a Philanthropist.

I have a heart for giving to those in need and leading my family in the act of giving purposefully and naturally.

I fully accept my role as a homemaker. I am diligent in this role.

My home is the center of creativity, productivity, and love for my family and anyone who walks through our doors.

Our seeds of giving have increase and abundance, in the lives of the people you've called us to give towards. Their needs are met in full. And they are now blessed to give to others, as well.

I decree and declare this over my life, as according to Proverbs 31:19-20

And it is so -- Amen.

# SOAP Scripture Study
# Day 9

## Video Lesson
https://proverbs31businesswoman.com/proverbs-31-woman-bible-study-day9

## Scripture
Write down today's focus scripture.

## Observation
What did you observe about the scripture that struck you?

## Application
How can you apply this deeper meaning, so that it has a heartfelt impact on your life?

## Prayer
Write out a prayer to God based upon what you just learned and where you'd like to grow, in your life.

# Notes & Journaling
# Day 9

# Notes & Journaling
# Day 9

# Notes & Journaling
# Day 9

# Reflections & Questions
## Day 9

1. In terms of your homemaking, how are you building your home? Reflect on Proverbs 14:1 and dig into ways you can be the wise woman who builds her home.

2. Are you purposeful in your giving to those in need? List some ways you can be more purposeful.

3. Consider creating a Legacy of Philanthropy for your family. Think of all the ways and places you can give to. Write them all down! No idea is too small or too big. Then begin a purposeful plan to start giving generously!

**DAY 10**

# Being Prepared For The Seasons In Life

### Proverbs 31:21-22

---

²¹ She is not afraid of snow for her household, for all her household are clothed in scarlet.

²² She makes bed coverings for herself; her clothing is fine linen and purple.

---

### CONFESSION OF TRUTH

I am discerning of the physical, emotional, and spiritual seasons of me and my family's life.

I am not afraid of the "winter" or lean seasons.

I am not surprised or caught off-guard because I am to be well-prepared and I help prepare my family and others around me.

I am modest and trendy. I dress with class and tastefulness.

People never have to wonder about the condition of my heart or relationship with Christ because of something I wear. My clothing choices reflect my heart and mostly the heart of God.

This does not mean I am put into a box. It simply means I am sensitive and discerning to the Holy Spirit's leading about my attire. I am confident He not only knows how to dress me but also how my clothing is "on-trend" for the personality and influence God's given me.

I am confident in this!

I decree and declare this over my life, as according to Proverbs 31:21-22

And it is so -- Amen.

# SOAP Scripture Study
# Day 10

## Video Lesson
https://proverbs31businesswoman.com/proverbs-31-woman-bible-study-day10

## Scripture
Write down today's focus scripture.

## Observation
What did you observe about the scripture that struck you?

## Application
How can you apply this deeper meaning, so that it has a heartfelt impact on your life?

## Prayer
Write out a prayer to God based upon what you just learned and where you'd like to grow, in your life.

# Notes & Journaling
# Day 10

# Notes & Journaling
# Day 10

# Notes & Journaling
# Day 10

# Reflections & Questions
# Day 10

1. How prepared are you and your family/household for the winter season (both physically and spiritually)?

2. Consider yourself in terms of modesty, how do you feel about the clothing you wear and the message it sends to others? Ask yourself this: "Do I allow the world to dress me or the Word of God?"

3. CHALLENGE!! Go through your closet and drawers, find any clothing that does not exhibit Godly modesty and either giveaway or discard. (Let the Holy Spirit nudge you.) I promise you'll feel a whole lot better about your clothing!

DAY 11

# Your Impact On Your Man
## Proverbs 31:23

---

²³ Her husband is known in the gates when he sits among the elders of the land.

---

### CONFESSION OF TRUTH

I am a respectful woman and (future) wife.

My character is Godly and points people towards Christ.

I love my (future) husband, therefore I chose to respect him and his God-given role in our family.

My (future) husband is highly esteemed and honored on his job, in the community, and any place he is known.

I am a powerful influence in his life. My good rubs off on him and bring goodness to his life.

I decree and declare this over my life, as according to Proverbs 31:23

And it is so -- Amen.

# SOAP Scripture Study
# Day 11

## Video Lesson
https://proverbs31businesswoman.com/proverbs-31-woman-bible-study-day11

## Scripture
Write down today's focus scripture.

## Observation
What did you observe about the scripture that struck you?

## Application
How can you apply this deeper meaning, so that it has a heartfelt impact on your life?

## Prayer
Write out a prayer to God based upon what you just learned and where you'd like to grow, in your life.

# Notes & Journaling
# Day 11

# Notes & Journaling
# Day 11

# Notes & Journaling
# Day 11

# Reflections & Questions
## Day 11

1. What causes a man to be respected among other men (especially those who are older, wiser, and respected in the community)?




2. Ask your husband what you can do to show him more respect. Write down what he says then commit to it. If it's a long list pick one or two things and focus on becoming better with those. (Don't overwhelm yourself!)




3. As you work on becoming a virtuous woman and desiring your husband to be respected among men, rate yourself on the following and make note of some areas where you can grow.

| Personal Assessment | Needs work = 0 | Excellent = 5 |
| --- | --- | --- |
| Health – Physical | | 0 1 2 3 4 5 |
| Health – Emotional/Mental | | 0 1 2 3 4 5 |
| Appearance | | 0 1 2 3 4 5 |
| Homemaking | | 0 1 2 3 4 5 |
| Love-making | | 0 1 2 3 4 5 |
| Honoring my husband before others | | 0 1 2 3 4 5 |

DAY 12

# The Freedom To Be Enterprising

*Proverbs 31:24-25*

---

$^{24}$ She makes linen garments and sells them; she delivers sashes to the merchant.

$^{25}$ Strength and dignity are her clothing, and she laughs at the time to come.

---

### CONFESSION OF TRUTH

I am a woman to honors her priorities and responsibilities.

I am confident in my skills and will be wise and diligent in using them to be enterprising to bless my family and impact Kingdom.

My profitability in my business and ministry is a direct reflection of the profitability in my home.

I am great at home; therefore I am great when I'm representing my home.

I am clothed with strength, dignity, and honor.

I am a living Epistle of Christ.

I have an attitude in a position of joy that only comes because Christ is at the center of it.

My smile radiates of this truth and permeates to others.

I decree and declare this over my life, as according to Proverbs 31:24-25

And it is so -- Amen.

# SOAP Scripture Study
# Day 12

## Video Lesson
https://proverbs31businesswoman.com/proverbs-31-woman-bible-study-day12

## Scripture
Write down today's focus scripture.

## Observation
What did you observe about the scripture that struck you?

## Application
How can you apply this deeper meaning, so that it has a heartfelt impact on your life?

## Prayer
Write out a prayer to God based upon what you just learned and where you'd like to grow, in your life.

# Notes & Journaling
# Day 12

# Notes & Journaling
# Day 12

# Notes & Journaling
# Day 12

# Reflections & Questions
# Day 12

1. What skills do you have that you could potentially use to be more enterprising? List ALL of your skills. You may be surprised!

2. What area do you need to work on and become more diligent? (Homemaking, care for family, care for yourself, respect for your husband, etc.)

3. What do people see when they see you? What do you want them to see?

**DAY 13**

# Speak Wisdom, Kindness, & Life!
### Proverbs 31:26-27

---

²⁶ She opens her mouth with wisdom,
and the teaching of kindness is on her tongue.

²⁷ She looks well to the ways of her household
and does not eat the bread of idleness.

---

### CONFESSION OF TRUTH

My mouth speaks wisdom, life, and kindness.

My words are purposeful and tell of my character and Godliness.

I do not gossip, backbite, slander, or compare myself to others.

I am changing the negative narrative of women, into the Godly, holy, and righteous purpose of women.

I am not an idle, busybody. I am so caught up in Jesus and God's plans for my life that there is no time to waste on non-essential activities or conversations.

I am a purposeful and intentional encourager of women.

My words give life and speak to the virtue of every woman I encounter.

I decree and declare this over my life, as according to Proverbs 31:26-27

And it is so -- Amen.

# SOAP Scripture Study
# Day 13

## Video Lesson
https://proverbs31businesswoman.com/proverbs-31-woman-bible-study-day13

## Scripture
Write down today's focus scripture.

## Observation
What did you observe about the scripture that struck you?

## Application
How can you apply this deeper meaning, so that it has a heartfelt impact on your life?

## Prayer
Write out a prayer to God based upon what you just learned and where you'd like to grow, in your life.

# Notes & Journaling
# Day 13

# Notes & Journaling
# Day 13

# Notes & Journaling
# Day 13

# Reflections & Questions
# Day 13

1. Think of a time when you did not use your mouth to speak wisdom and kindness. What was the outcome? How could you have done something differently?

2. Evaluate yourself on how you use your mouth with your family, close friends, and others.

| "Mouth-Gate" Assessment: | Never = 0    Often = 5 |
|---|---|
| Gossip | 0 1 2 3 4 5 |
| Unkind words | 0 1 2 3 4 5 |
| Encouraging words | 0 1 2 3 4 5 |
| Listen before speaking | 0 1 2 3 4 5 |
| Flattery | 0 1 2 3 4 5 |
| Praise | 0 1 2 3 4 5 |

3. List all of the tasks for your household. Schedule out one day of work and assign every member of your household to specific tasks. Hopefully, you'll see that your hands are full and your household should be your main priority.

DAY 14

# Let Your Children & Husband Praise You!

## Proverbs 31:28-29

---

⁲⁸ Her children rise up and call her blessed; her husband also, and he praises her:

²⁹ "Many women have done excellently, but you surpass them all."

---

### CONFESSION OF TRUTH

My husband and children rise and call me blessed.

My good works and character speak of my relationship with God.

Outside of God the only opinions and praise that matter are those of my family and who I share my life with.

My mind and heart are set on not only my end-of-life legacy, by on my Living Legacy. I am busy living a life worth living through Jesus the Christ.

I choose to "work on me more than I work on others." I have no time to point fingers, criticize, or to compare. My time is well-spent on growing, pruning, and maturing in my own life.

My life glorifies, honors, and pleases the Lord.

I decree and declare this over my life, as according to Proverbs 31:28-29

And it is so -- Amen.

# SOAP Scripture Study
# Day 14

## Video Lesson
https://proverbs31businesswoman.com/proverbs-31-woman-bible-study-day14

## Scripture
Write down today's focus scripture.

## Observation
What did you observe about the scripture that struck you?

## Application
How can you apply this deeper meaning, so that it has a heartfelt impact on your life?

## Prayer
Write out a prayer to God based upon what you just learned and where you'd like to grow, in your life.

# Notes & Journaling
# Day 14

# Notes & Journaling
# Day 14

# Notes & Journaling
# Day 14

# Reflections & Questions
# Day 14

Consider the legacy you want to live in and leave for your family. Think of the kinds of things you want your husband and children to say about you RIGHT NOW while you are alive! List them here. Then decide the areas you need to grow in and the areas you are doing GREAT in! Ask yourself:

**What do I do well?**

**Where do I need to grow?**

**What actionable steps can I take to become a more virtuous woman?**

(I've left you plenty of space to write today!)

DAY 15

# The One Thing That Matters Most (Eternity)

### Proverbs 31:30-31

---

$^{30}$ Charm is deceitful, and beauty is vain,
but a woman who fears the Lord is to be praised.

$^{31}$ Give her of the fruit of her hands,
and let her works praise her in the gates.

---

### CONFESSION OF TRUTH

I am a Proverbs 31 Woman.

I am a woman who fears the Lord.

I delight myself, in the Lord.

I seek after eternal rewards.

My sole purpose on earth is to walk with God intimately and purposefully.

Living a life poured out for Jesus is the biggest Legacy I can establish and leave in the earth. I have set out to do just that.

The Lord will give me the fruit of my hands! My eternal rewards are GREAT!

I decree and declare this over my life, as according to Proverbs 31:30-31

And it is so -- Amen.

# SOAP Scripture Study
# Day 15

## Video Lesson

https://proverbs31businesswoman.com/proverbs-31-woman-bible-study-day15

## Scripture

Write down today's focus scripture.

## Observation

What did you observe about the scripture that struck you?

## Application

How can you apply this deeper meaning, so that it has a heartfelt impact on your life?

## Prayer

Write out a prayer to God based upon what you just learned and where you'd like to grow, in your life.

# Notes & Journaling
# Day 15

# Notes & Journaling
# Day 15

# Notes & Journaling
# Day 15

# Reflections & Questions
# Day 15

1. How has your perspective of the Virtuous Woman written about in Proverbs 31 changed since starting this study?

2. On Day 1 of our study, you took a simple survey, evaluating yourself in certain key areas of virtuous character. Take the time to re-evaluate where you are now, at the end of our bible study. How have your grown?

| Scriptural knowledge of following: | 0 = immature | 5 = mature |
|---|---|---|
| Fear of God | 0 1 2 3 4 5 | |
| Holiness | 0 1 2 3 4 5 | |
| Wisdom | 0 1 2 3 4 5 | |
| Sow-Reap Law | 0 1 2 3 4 5 | |

| Personal maturity in godly character: | 0 = immature | 5 = mature |
|---|---|---|
| Trustworthiness | 0 1 2 3 4 5 | |
| Control of tongue | 0 1 2 3 4 5 | |
| Humility | 0 1 2 3 4 5 | |
| Wisdom | 0 1 2 3 4 5 | |
| Peace of mind | 0 1 2 3 4 5 | |
| Diligence | 0 1 2 3 4 5 | |
| Benevolence | 0 1 2 3 4 5 | |
| Health and appearance | 0 1 2 3 4 5 | |
| Excellence | 0 1 2 3 4 5 | |

# You're All Done!

Thank you for being bold enough and open enough to go with me all the way to the end of this bible study! It takes quite a bit of dedication and sacrifice. But you, my SisterFriend, did it!!

Not only am I proud of you, but so is God!

I'd love to know how this Bible Study has impacted your life. **Please tell me what you learned, what you loved, and what you would like to see more of!**

You can send me a quick email to hello@proverbs31businesswoman.com or drop a note on my Facebook, Instagram, or Pinterest pages.

facebook.com/angelicakduncan

instagram.com/angelicakduncan

pinterest.com/angelicakduncan

I can't wait to hear from you!

**Dance with the King!**

*Angelica*

Made in United States
North Haven, CT
22 August 2023

40617525R00072